Copyright © 2025 by Raine Ménard

All rights reserved. No part of this book may be reproduced in any manner whatsoever without written permission except in the case of brief quotations embodied in critical articles and reviews.

First Printing, 2025

MYSTERIOUS WORKINGS OF
THE TEENAGE BRAIN

MYSTERIOUS WORKINGS OF THE TEENAGE BRAIN

RAINE MÉNARD

. . .

I bet my soul is a marble
it's pretty funky
and it won't stop rolling around

For those who don't understand it themselves...

and for all the friends I've left behind.
I love you all

Intro

This teenage girl controls half of me
a parasite I have to see
impulsive and dangerous energy
destructive, walking felony
my higher self is trying to take her on
but this feisty bitch fights me
yin and yang of who I am
controls me

List of Poems

After Class
Mystic Garden
My First Man was Beige
365
Madly
Friday Night
Parasite
Energy Lords in Different Sides of the Sky
Mom's House
Untitled
Purple Lung
Wake the F*ckkk Uppppp!!!
4:22
Our Father
Morticians are Horny Too
All League No Legends
Broken Homes Don't Exist
Street Junk
Thursday 11:54pm
Young Love
Happy Orphan
Deep Rest
This Bitch Who Runs Away
Realizing That Shit Doesn't Work

Eating my Tail for Lunch
My Princess Tale
Unfinished Basement
Strung Out
Holy Boy
Rigor Mortis
Prequel
I Can't Have a Girlfriend
Pacific Air
2am
September
Love or Doom
False Fate
Plague
Assholes
Blue Tapestry
Friends, Right?
Grade 12 is Making me Too Edgy
This Book. Right Now.
All I Know is Fuck All.
Human Compost
Beginning of the End
Why am I an Emotional Masochist
Obsessive
Distraction is Free
Big and Thin
Lurk
Last Call

Authors Note

Next to me lies six journals filled front to back with hundreds of poems I have spewed out over the years. I couldn't stop writing.

It made me feel sane or comfortable with my insanity.

That hasn't changed.

This book is a collection of those six.

I spent most of my youth alone, aching for a far away land. There was *nothing* I wanted more then to get the fuck out of Thunder Bay. The music scene felt non existent and that's what I ached for the most. Surrounded by people my age, I never felt like I could be myself. I wanted to escape this "normal" life with minimal artistic opportunity.

When I was 14 I made myself a promise: the second I turn 18 I'm fucking leaving. That's exactly what I did.

People often told me that moving to Vancouver at such a young age was some sort of "courageous" or a "bold" thing to do.

Bullshit.

I've been preparing for this shit for 4 years.

The funny thing about moving is, at some point, it makes you appreciate your hometown. There are days I would do anything to be in the middle of a pristine lake in Dryden, or sit in my beautiful backyard in Thunder Bay. I miss my friends and family dearly.

About half of what I wrote was in a marijuana induced paradise (or anxiety) in the front entrance of my mom's house. The sanctity of this time was dedicated to falling deeply in love with music and writing my heart out. It gave me so much hope and longing. Feeding myself delusion was one of the best things I've ever done.

I hope that you find these pages relatable, funny or vaguely entertaining. Most of all I hope they make you feel something: anger, sadness, disgust or maybe understanding.

After Class

I cannot handle my misery.
is this how it's supposed to be?
blindfolded behind the wheel
smashing on the gas
I know the crash is coming,
but it feels so free to go fast

Winded up and wound down
all in one hour
there's no lively injection
quite like the downer

I want my words to be heard
your blood to feel
I'll spend my days transforming tragic
so you can strip me down
these naked feelings
impossible to steal

Mystic Garden

I'm on fairies last breath
and there's nothing left

I need time to feed
these demons inside of me

my gift is a curse
walking around with this abortion in my purse

My First Man Was Beige

Being with you makes me feel alone.
My house still smells like you
I just want to wash it away

It seems I needed something to do
I guess that someone was you
I'm never going to get that time back

fuck.

365

Four-bedroom walls are my hell
barriers that confine me
taunt me with what could be

nonetheless:
these walls give me life
creating endless possibilities to mold

being locked and taunted
motivated to work
to dig my way out

the life I will live is thanks to these walls.

Tough love.

Madly

Everything I do
I want to do madly
to give all of me
to bleed all over your feeling

I want to rip my heart out
and serve it warm
for you all to dig in
with your knives and forks

every hell I go through
I want to wrap it up and give it to you.

It's my present

Friday Night

As I stand in the bathroom mirror
and fix my hair
I am reminded no one will ever love me
the way I love myself

Parasite

I fall in and out
a thousand times a day
unable to understand
what all the voices say

some break-in
some too rash
they're battling it out in contrast

tossing and turning from left to right
both so strong
but one has a sharper bite

controlled by my compass
spinning steadfast
shooting around
maybe I'm crazy
I blast

are you ruled by the voices in your stomach?

Energy Lords in Different Sides of the Sky

Your words are perfectly placed
marveled when understood
my words are painfully birthed
constant impulsive pregnancy

so you stay among this bloody mess
so high up perched
I'm flailing away from the rest

I'll climb your ladder
nearly debris amongst the ground
I don't know if I jumped or fell
I can never tell

Mom's House

My dad would freak
if he knew what I do
my lies keep the peace

they don't want to come back
I'm their unfinished art
now I'm scribbling with crayons

visions distorted
will of a disciple
with questionable morals

Untitled

I want to be your rug
but I bet I'd never get clean
marinating in that dream

Purple Lung

My heart so heavy
she cries for relief
once she holds you down
you wish you'd never leave

so here I am once again
destroyed from nothing at all
I can never understand
how I got here

how can one not get sick of themselves?

What kind of fate is this
so good at running
but can't sit down
so good at living fast
but can't look around

Wake the Fuckkk Uppppp!!!

I wake up in a daze
resonated
I want to make them fucking hate it

let's go
bust it open smooth
pack the bowl,
pass the light,
my youth

died twice
working on three
tripping on my bones
love is just fucking and getting stoned

guess which one is my home
guess where I find my truth
not in someone's body
there's no use

so dead set
far removed
I'm gone
situation diffused

4:22

I'm not in pain
just a bruised chronic smoker
I fear your loss of self
how easily you sell your soul to illusion

following a road of yellow bricks
sidelined by many men I could fix
I don't need the strain

uniquely needed by myself
my lover
and personal hell
my head stays down
torn from the world around

Our Father

Preacher in purple
victim to intrusive thought
cause the god he prays is everything he's got.

Vowing away pussy
for pages in a book
can the government money
sustain his outlook?
He can't help but dwell
maybe he's not coming back

Parishioners bow down
to an empty man
faith stale
like the bread in his hand

Angels once terrorized a man at rest
the dawn and young hope
washed away
the priest and his rope

Morticians are Horny Too

My head turns off more than on
confused disgruntled feelings
my heart is cold
like the hands of a mortician
but here I stand
wanting to be set on fire

All League. No Legends.

In between my thighs
questions your sincerity
you don't belong to me
full of ambiguity

this cat is cautious
dark eyes admire your design
you're in the mountains
I'm in the forest
different words of different poets
reviewing intentions in time

Broken Homes Don't Exist

Bad kids in bad worlds
filled with love and pain
kids that lived too young
cope in different ways

my mother coped
in an empty apartment
seated on milk crates
my father plunged into empty love
to fill himself

bad kids
in bad worlds
surrounded by humans
now doing what humans do

Street Junk

It's so loud
I can't hear a motherfucking thing
constant rumble
sirens screech
I can't run
and I can't stay
maybe it's always been this way
moments on ice have turned me purple
and I have to keep digging in this never-ending world
where no one is living.

Thursday 11:54pm

Beep beep
fucking beep
another night
I don't sleep
I never depend
cause I'm failed time and time
and again

I splatter my deviation
like a kid splatters paint
I always liked the wicked witch
and hoped she stole that baby
I relate to her anger
and hold no sympathy

cause distress in a perfect world that doesn't exist
in a perfect world that doesn't rest
let me be the antagonist

Young Love

Your impulsivity grows
as I lie next to you
you need to tell me
if I make you crazy
if the thought of losing me
sends a sharp pain
throughout any internal organs

a divine woman makes you feel a man
and there's many:
every
but no one quite like me
you can search every country
and every bloody sea
this sharp set of circumstance
burns way too deep
if love is a drug
I want to be fucking heroin

Happy Orphan

There's a broken sink and a broken home
a family room filled with people
but someone sits alone

Imposter back to roaming the streets
silver angels silently play
it's all a washed milky array

floating alone
drifting back to my lease
it's all guessing
embrace the defeat

life is the longest vacation you painfully beat.

Deep Rest

I'm a towel hanging on a dangly hook
sopping.
dripping wet.
left to dry.
once I do
I'm wet and reused

sagging on this hook
I am sick of myself
my blue fibers droop
yet I mold with an attitude

wrap me up and roll me around
whirling in the washing machine

taken out
mostly dried
laying on a shelf
until she breaks and cries
I drip.
I drop.
I weep.
yet I'm exactly who I need to be

This Bitch Who Runs Away

I think this place is going to torment me
2 sides of a window
one life on one end,
plenty on the other

I watch feet pass all-day
mothers,
drunken lovers
but after midnight
when life has gone away
I sit as the watcher of South Main
the perfect view of another dinky café

this was everything I've ever wanted
sometimes it breaks my heart
the dynamics of everything I don't have on one end
and consistency on the other

Realizing that Shit Doesn't Work

Big worlds don't cater to those who run fast
the same ball of energy
can spend all day on an airplane
to find out
they can't outrun themselves

I think I'm okay with that.

You can spend your whole life trying to escape
I'd rather outrun everything else
just to keep myself

Eating my Tail for Lunch

I'm waiting for the depression to set in
comfort in fear
how the fuck did I even end up here.

Free but transparent
happiness feels dull when I'm in it
and I just can't recognize
you're either my savior or hell
I'm too fucking naive to tell

My Princess Tale

A dead man's prize
mashed in the peel
paralyzed tantric ordeal
running around
head cut off
dangling participles can feel

spinning on toads
splashing around in my moat
mud immerses my feet
suddenly I can't breathe

Old Moon runs in heels to a feast
concrete full of yellow lines
no street to turn east

Full Moon strips to feed
she dances all night long
yet she's the last to eat

Unfinished Basement

I love rock bottom because it hurts when I land
I am a portal of mortal perception
blind to my reflection
dancing in the ripples
of this 5th world dimension

can't see my hands
but I grab
can't feel my arms
but I crawl
I ache for days but waste them all
what am I but a freefall

Strung Out

Burnout is my practice
pot is my hero
not meant to stop
but fucking go
chill
but never slow
unwound and running late
desperate
trying to make it to the show
emotion is the key to success
loneliness is a mothers love
unable to dissolve to sense
embracing temporary power
me and the spliff in my nightstand
partners in crime

Rigor Mortis

It's all so prophetic
I'm immune
normalized tantric wounds

from now on it's the lady picture show
maybe I'm doing just fine
destructive side addicted to temptation
rigor mortis

Prequel

At the end of a day
I did the best I could
I am not at fault
for my distress
this one's on you
tired of doing things I'm not supposed to

now I don't know
but my cards are played
it's your turn to go

I fade to black
what was put out
was not sent back
I need your understanding
the prequel was so beautiful
I don't want to let her go
the amazing talent
was all before the show

why can't I be the one you want
see me through the shell I use
tragic abuse of the heart
so far from the trees
when will I find peace

Holy Boy

You weren't for me
I admired your beauty
that did not resonate
temporary bliss

you do not understand
who you're fucking with
you should see what I manage
he had a distorted view

I'm the devil's temptation
born to stop him from praying
but I really don't give a fuck.

I Can't Have a Girlfriend

She was drugs.
the bag of dope under my sink
cause when she hit I flew
I'm sorry I left
it's what I had to do
she was going to stab me
unaware of the tendencies
searching for someone you can't keep
I'd let you ruin my life

I want to run away with you
young promise
the sun to my moon
but you don't want to
freedom isn't on your list
that's okay
maybe it's not your shit
one but separate
the ying has to ying
and the yang has to yang

Pacific Air

I'm so heavy
deep in my chest
and on this chest
your head rests

it must be so warm
smoke wafts in
stale air from the city street
I lay doused in the soft aroma

home has felt true for the first time
in a while
I reminisce
I exhale
I'm bringing this puzzle piece
this warm handsome glow
back home

2am

Safe in the absence of light
instead of blazing under the sun
silence in the moon
is where I'm meant to be
nighttime and minor keys
psychedelic tea
makes me feel like me

September

Maybe I'm just putting things together
harvest moon
perfect weather
I don't think I could ever love you
the way the wind and the trees
love me

Love or Doom

I'm never-ending doomed.
I want to try
give it a whirl
I'm painting with dark colors
for the first time in a hundred moons
I have nothing to say
too much going in
no exit
blind in a path and wrecks it
stretch and dissect it
abominable death threats
let go
or protect it

False Fate

The darkest clouds are coming to Earth
filling up the sky
who holds this brush
painting our world under a black cloak
gaping disease
drowning these men from underneath
dissolving pit
melting inwards throughout the stomach
then they leave
devastating plummet
blood poured out
covering every unfortunate bystander

Plague

I'm starving out parts of myself to feed you
bleeding through my missing skin
lungs are drowning blue

grating my teeth through the gravel
I lost my voice
invisible tongue

the walls are getting closer
ceiling caving in
it's at my neck now
bending down
I just want it to end me

I can't wait to feel the light as I'm born again

Assholes

Humans spew garbage at each other
we're all full of shit
sinners of the free world

I'm sorry to all my fellow passengers
I was just being human
no intention to hurt or cause harm

I'm just fucking up a little
we all fuck up a little

right?

Blue Tapestry

The outside world isn't real
just the disks and tracks
kept on my inside walls
I dedicate myself
to the sanctity of this world
the place I belong
who I am

I'm going to be here forever
I wish the world would just slow down

Friends, Right?

I can't follow you
and you can't follow me
I treaded too long in the sun
in this new world order
I am numb
I follow a different path
the moonlight misses me as I drift back
do you miss it back?

Grade 12 is Making Me Too Edgy

Haven't had time to feel
progression of what's real
lost in this realm
I missed the falling of the tree
that's not usually like me

it's just sex I can't feel
I'm vibrating somewhere else
it's quite the ordeal
suddenly I fall home

I can't take this shit so seriously

living in secrecy
eight separate lives
eyes giving out
not surprised
the wind changes
blinded without stability
waiting to land in a whole new world

unpredictability humbles me
challenges me

This Book. Right Now.

Maybe I should write a book with pages no one will read
empty my soul with pen and dreams
cash rules everything
and this I despise
life isn't money
why should I be surprised?
I've got so much to do
someone to be
and I've got this world
flourishing around me
cash is cruel
so I write to ease my fright
every word placed with such care
who knows
maybe I'll print and press if I dare

All I Know is Fuck All.

Delusional consumption
walking in the brain

writing
on the hundredth meridian
driving west
probably going insane

maybe I'm going to hell
I genuinely cannot tell

Human Compost

I belong in the dirt more than anywhere else in this world
the more I learn
the more I live
I am from the rib of Mother Earth

the more I drown
the better I swim
beloved daughter
listen past your limbs

tap into the worldly wisdom
that has watered you

you bloom and pass
after every snowfall
while your roots always grow deeper

Beginning of the End

I wish the world would swallow us up
may the black clouds reverse rain
tearing all of our possessions away
I'm okay to go
because I'll watch you dissolve with me

Why Am I An Emotional Masochist

Why do I torture myself?
Why do I crave to be hollow?
This internal drama is self inflicted and rigid
I like to feel my heart burn
I miss the sensation of a drastic blow
dropping my eyes
torturing my soul
opening wounds just to watch them drip
this is why I'm a masochist.
Why don't I ever get over myself?
I sink the way I used to
I'm a child again
I like to feel in danger
not often,
but sometimes
I want to feel absolutely helpless
to be abused by someone besides myself
left alone and beat down
in a desperate state
just so I know
someone can hurt me
brutally
someone besides myself
then maybe
I can give myself sympathy

Obsessive

Tempted to dive head first into a world of my own creation
not always in the best way
I want to make myself hurt
to use all my might
to dig up everything that makes me uncomfortable
and swim in it
and drink it
and breathe it
it's not good for me
but I want to be rocked off course
disassembled and taunted
just so I can feel desperate and lame
a copy who can be compared
I hate that feeling

and I hate that it makes me want more.

Distraction is Free

Demons like you on outside walls
this way you'll never face them head-on
they'll suck you out
watch you consume yourself

I am water for a thousand trees
every root grows deeper in search of me
sometimes I'm a falling leaf
no hesitation
carried away in the breeze

I fall and turn red
sometimes it's calm
sometimes it's not calm at all
but whenever I'm picked up and on a drift
I just fall back and enjoy the trip

Big and Thin

My psychedelic adventure
feels better than ever
same step
same stoop
pondering all these endeavors
on this step
born and raised
with grated teeth
a ghost town slave
here's to another day
baby riot
scream it out
everyone's quiet
sloppy story
get out
divorce me
leave me crying and horny
I'm the crack in your concrete
dancing
tight
dark
and discrete

Lurk

I want more
containing the elements of bore
slowing yourself
is an element of more

you'll catch me slipping
I'm an emotional whore
I debated getting faded
but here we are

Oh Sweet Nothing is so much to adore
my pen is my only friend
in this big wide world

the bench warmer can tell you how to play
admiration of this violent display
happily hidden away

she lurks in the world by choice
study and mastery are uniquely her voice
unenrol from societies lie

Last Call

I'm so excited for the last call
will I be released or contained
the final display of truth
why give a fuck when I see the fate anyways
all for a reason
the shades of different seasons
I'm just being me
fuck all who can't see
this girl keeps growing
too much faith makes me sick
the time has come
to go back where I came from
you never took me there

understanding the concept of unfair
I just want to steer
I'll have myself
back in the futures place I dwell
the fucked up mind
creators hell
don't waste your energy
squeezing blood from a stone

so much easier said then done.

... ~ 57

...

58 ~ ...

Now you're just a slave to the pages in my book.

www.ingramcontent.com/pod-product-compliance
Lightning Source LLC
Chambersburg PA
CBHW020342010526
44119CB00048B/568